Trade Secrets of a
  Haircolor Expert

Presents

Haircolor 101
The Beginning

D1609301

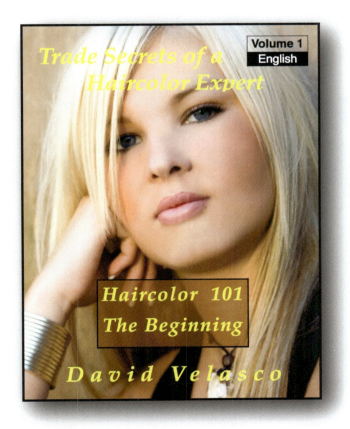

TCC South

Crowley Learning Center

David Velasco

Disclaimer

This course is designed to educate and inform its readers of the subject matter covered herein. The publisher and author do not warrant any guarantee or responsibility to any person or entity with respect to any loss or damage caused directly or indirectly by the information contained in this book. The reader is expressly warned to consider and adopt all safety precautions that might be indicated by the activities herein and to avoid all potential hazards. By following the instructions contained herein, the reader willingly assumes all risk and liability in connection with such instructions.

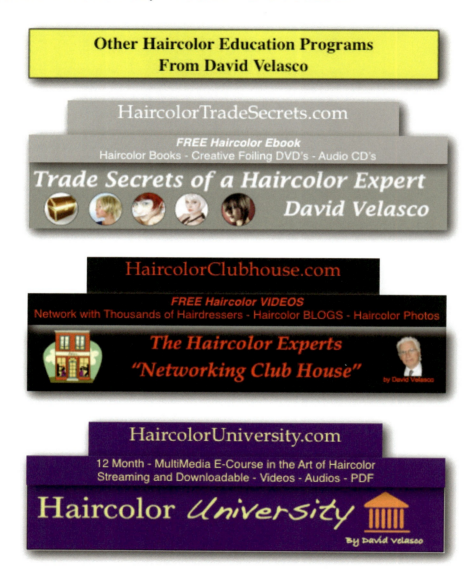

WHAT INDUSTRY LEADERS ARE SAYING ABOUT "TRADE SECRETS"

In the early 1990s, I made this decision to switch to Wella Hair exclusively for the Bumble and bumble salon. As we had been using a mixture of 4/5 hair color brands, this was an extremely difficult transition. At that time, we had nine colorists and we were one of the busiest salons in New York. The first week of transition was extremely difficult with everyone completely confused and the results were varied.

It was at this point that I first met David Velasco. He had just finished a long stint as the art director and head colorist for Wella US and he very much wanted to come work at Bumble. I hired him specifically to try and help us make sense of this new color methodology that we were going to be using. With David's help, things changed and improved almost immediately. Apart from his quiet leadership and charismatic way, he was simply never ruffled. Further, he has a very deep understanding of the basic concepts of hair color as well as the complex tasks that some clients choose to do. He managed very quickly to make sure that all nine colorists were confident in the new haircolor and made sure they continued to broaden the skills and knowledge that they were missing and strengthen their techniques. His overall personality and experience were huge boosts to a salon that had over 120 employees.

After five years, David decided to return to his own salon. However, he had made an indelible mark on the quality of work that our hair color department was able to produce. I would say that every salon in America should have this book series. It is a must read, must know, must study book.

Michael A. Gordon
Founder
Bumble and bumble

David
When you told me that you were writing a book I knew that it would be good, but what you wrote is the encyclopedia of haircolor!

Dee Levin
Salon Nornandee
Secretary of Intercoiffure-America

Dear David,

I was reading your book again tonight. I must say, you have some INCREDIBLE CONTENT! You have a FABULOUS OPPORTUNITY to set a higher tone for haircolor education.

I think this book could set a new standard for "Non-manufacturer" education. You have done an EXQUISITE job writing a truly definitive work.
Again, your content is PHENOMENAL!
Wishing you all the very best! Stay in touch, -- you are on to something very special. This shows what a wonderful teacher you are.

Beth!

Beth Minardi

David,

I have just finished the first four chapters of your book and I must tell you that it is one of the best haircolor books I have ever seen.

One of the easiest to follow, great comments on the 'trade secrets', non commercial, and it is very obvious that you have a lot of knowledge and experience on haircolor from being behind the chair.

I look forward to reading the rest of the book and to seeing you in September

Fondly,
Sheila

Sheila Zaricor
Treasurer - International Haircolor Exchange

WHAT YOU WILL LEARN IN THIS BOOK   Pg.

Introduction

<u>Knowledge is Power</u>

Knowledge is power. This power is having confidence in your skills and abilities as a professional haircolorist - the power to create beauty and make people feel great about themselves; the power to distinguish yourself as an authority in your field and gain praise and recognition from your peers and community. And, of course, this power translates into increasing your income according to your expertise.

Yes, I know all of this can come true for you. How do I know? Because it happened to me and I have seen it happen to many hairdressers to whom I have had the pleasure of teaching these techniques and strategies over my forty years in the beauty industry.

You hold in your hands the power to achieve all of this and more.

Napoleon Hill, famed author of one of the best personal achievement book ever written, *Think and Grow Rich,* called this type of knowledge "Specialized Knowledge" and it is #4 in his history-making book.

He goes on to say that Specialized Knowledge is the kind that inspired people like Henry Ford and Thomas Edison to go on and achieve greatness in their lifetimes. This type of greatness cannot be achieved with only general knowledge.

I am not saying that once you have studied this course, you will become the next Bill Gates of haircolor, but once you read and internalize the information in this course, it does have the power to change your career and your life forever.

Why This Course is Titled:
Trade Secrets of a Haircolor Expert

Webster's Dictionary defines TRADE SECRET as:

Main Entry: **trade secret**
Function: *noun*
something (as a formula) which has economic value to a business because it is not generally known or easily discoverable by observation.

The Wikipedia online encyclopedia defines TRADE SECRET as:

A **trade secret** is a formula, practice, process, design, or compilation of information used by a business to obtain an advantage over competitors.

In this course, you will learn many formulation concepts that are not generally known by the masses of hairdressers. Sure, some of them will seem familiar to you and you may have heard them somewhere along the line in your training. However, hearing something and learning how to use what you have heard are two very different things.

The main thing that is going to set you apart from your competition, giving you the status and recognition as a Haircolor Expert in your community is knowledge, not just any kind of knowledge, but, as stated before, "Specialized Knowledge".

You can only get this kind of knowledge two ways - by learning from trial and error (this will take years) or by learning from someone that has been there before you. Specialized Knowledge will not be found in the textbooks in our industry or by going to weekend hair shows designed to entertain hairdressers and sell products.

When I first started to learn haircolor, well-known hair colorists at that time used to keep their formulations under lock and key. They literally had metal strong boxes where they kept their client color cards so no one could steal their formulas.

Today things are different. Most haircolorists are willing to share their ideas and color concepts with others. But the question now becomes - whose way is right; whose way is best and who's willing to guide me step-by-step through every haircolor procedure until I have the confidence to go it alone?

In this course, you will find the Trade Secrets that will give you the confidence to go it alone, and, as a side benefit, you will also shave many years off your learning curve. Instead of taking years and learning by trial and error, you will be able to refer back to this information over and over again throughout your career.

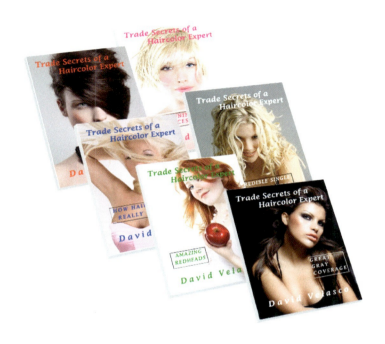

How to Use This Course

This course is laid out in a progressive knowledge-based sequence.

The first two volumes, *Haircolor 101- The Beginning* and *How Haircolor Really Works*, are "must read" books. The information in these two books must be understood before moving on to the other books. In these books, you will learn the theories, techniques and strategies that I will refer to over and over as you progress through the rest of the course.

Also, if you are experiencing gray coverage problems, I highly recommend reading Volume 3, *Great Gray Coverage* next. In this book you will learn 9 strategies for covering gray hair as well as how to work with gray hair in every conceivable situation.

After you have studied these three books, feel free to jump around to the other books as you wish.

In each of the other books, you will find an introduction to that particular segment of the course, followed by special formulation strategies that will guarantee you success in performing every possible haircolor situation. Towards the end of each chapter, is a color correction section that will guide you, step-by-step through any haircolor problem that you will ever encounter.

In this color correction section, you will not only learn **how** to fix every haircolor problem you will ever encounter, but you will also learn **why** this problem occurred and **how to prevent** it from happening in the future.

Also, so that colorists around the world can utilize this course, no specific product name or shade is mentioned. Instead, in each haircolor situation in this course, every effort has been made to refer to the formulation by **level** & **tone** only. Therefore, it doesn't matter what haircolor manufacturer or brand name you are using, you will still be able to utilize all the information in this course.

Once you have internalized this information, you will see your creativity expand, feel your confidence grow and be well on your way to becoming a haircolor specialist and a true expert in the field.

I truly wish you much success in your journey of becoming a haircolor expert and I would love to hear from you about your success along the way. Also, if you happen to encounter a haircolor situation that you cannot find the answer to in this course, please don't hesitate to email me at david@dvsalon.com and I will gladly assist you in any way I can.

I wish you massive success in all your haircolor endeavors,

David Velasco

PS: As a thank you for purchesing this book, I would like to give you a FREE 128 Page Haircolor E-Book, 7 Steps to Haircolor Mastery. To download it, go to:

www.HaircolorTradeSecrets.com

10

Introduction

So what is it about coloring hair that makes "haircolor" so complicated?

Before I begin, I just want to tell you that I too was at one time totally confused about hair color. It's a matter of fact, I was so afraid of doing haircolor that I would send my customers to other hairdressers to get their hair colored, or I would even try to talk them out of getting color in fear of losing them to other hairdressers.

But then one day I decided that if others could color hair so could I. After all it's not brain surgery and I knew many hairdressers who were no smarter or no better than me who were achieving great results with haircolor every day.

I believe that one of the things that makes haircolor so complicated is that you don't just have to learn one thing, like cutting a "Bob". You have to learn a multiple of 4 components that work together to get the finished result.

Those four components are:

1- *The secrets of the* **HAIR**

2- *The secrets of the* **PRODUCTS**

3- *The secrets of* **FORMULATION**

4- *The secrets of* **APPLICATION *and* TIMING**

There are actually 5, if you also consider how to conduct a ***haircolor consultation***, but we will just stay with the actual service for now.

So let's begin………

4 Keys to Haircolor

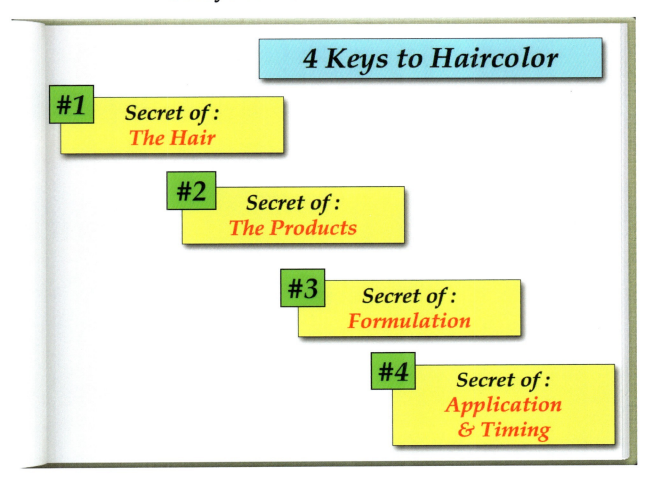

This book is divided into 4 key areas. First we're going to talk about the "secrets of the hair", what is the hair like: texture, porosity, natural Level, underlying pigment, etc.

Next we will discuss the secrets of the products - Temporary haircolor, Semi-Permanent haircolor, Demi Haircolor and Permanent haircolor. We will discuss how different they are, where in the hair they live, etc.

Then we will talk about the secrets of formulating haircolor. We will look at 2 types of Tonal Systems, how to use the swatch book, haircolor tones and bases and the color wheel.

And finally, we will put it all together by explaining the application and timing of a haircolor service.

Okay let's go to the first one, *The Secrets of the Hair,* the first key to understanding haircolor.

Key#1 -- The Secrets of the Hair

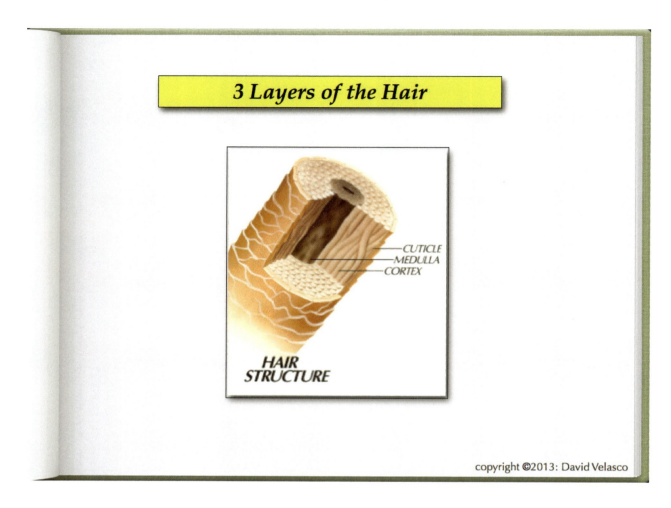

3 Layers of the Hair

CUTICLE
MEDULLA
CORTEX

HAIR STRUCTURE

Beauty school basics teach us that the hair is made up of 3 different layers. The outer layer is the cuticle layer, the center is the cortex, and the very middle is called the medulla.

In the world of haircolor, the only 2 layers that we are really concerned about are the first 2 - the cuticle layer (on the outside) and the cortex. The medulla doesn't play any active role in haircolor. As matter of fact, scientists propose that the only reason for the medulla is that it has some insulation properties. Animals like bears and dogs have very thick medullas for insulation. Many people today don't even have medullas. It appears that it is wearing away over time.

In any case, most of the haircolor action really takes place in the center- in the cortex layer. The cuticle layer plays an important role because the cuticle protects the inside layer (cortex) so it has to be in great condition. If the cuticle becomes damaged as in dry, bridle hair, it cannot protect the cortex layer and the hair will become overly porous and hair that's overly porous cannot hold good haircolor.

> **Haircolor Secret**
>
> Good haircolor can only exist in healthy hair. No matter what kind of conditioners or hair repair methods you do, if the cuticle layer has been torn off, nothing is going to replace it. Therefore, creating good haircolor will be impossible.

The best way to think of the cuticle layer protecting the cortex layer is to imagine a tree. The cuticle layer is like the bark of a tree in that it protects the inside of the tree. The inside of the tree has fibers and sap.

So, what the bark (cuticle) does for the tree (hair) is protects the sap from drying out. As long as the sap is moist, the tree is alive and it can bend with the wind. It's flexible, and it's vibrant.

But if you take a hatchet and hack off all the bark, all of a sudden all that sap starts to dry out in the tree. The tree becomes brittle. And the first time a strong wind comes along, the tree will crack and break. It won't bend anymore.

Well, the same thing with hair. At all costs, we have to protect the inside of the hair with the cuticle layer. The cuticle layer is like the bark of the tree, and it protects the hair itself.

When the hair is damaged through chemical processes like bleaching, perming or too much work with hot irons, flatirons or through environmental damage like sun bleached or too much salt water or chlorine pool water, the cuticle becomes very damaged.

When the cuticle gets damaged, it breaks off. It actually chips off. It is like shingles falling off of an old roof. And when this happens the cortex (the inside layer of the hair) becomes exposed to the elements and then the hair dries out.

The hair doesn't have sap of course but there is a type of substance that binds the fiber bundles together. Scientists call this cement like substance". I have also heard it called "Amorphous Glue", whatever that is, but in any case you get the picture.

When we work with haircolor, we are in the business of controlling damage to a certain degree. In other words, all haircolor is going to damage the hair to a certain degree when an oxidative tint is used. This does not happen for all haircolor, only an oxidative tint.

I want to stress that whenever you do a haircolor service, always try to use the most gentle product first to do the job. That is what will keep the cuticle layer intact. As long as the cuticle layer is intact, then good color can be achieved. Good color can never hold on hair that has been damaged.

One other important point about a cuticle layer is that a lot of people think a cuticle layer are like shingles on a roof or like scales on a fish. This analogy is used all the time (I used it myself in the last paragraph), because it comes close to that. But it is not like individual little scales like on a fish. It's actually one large scale that wraps itself around like a cylinder around the hair as it grows. So, it continues to wrap itself around. It's not individual little layers.

This is important because, if the cuticle layer gets damaged, the result is split ends or dry hair. If the cuticle area is damaged and it isn't cut off, that cuticle layer will eventually "unravel" its way up the hair shaft.

Have you ever seen someone with long hair and she has little flyaway stray hairs coming off their head? This is because, instead of cutting the ends, like should have been done, as the hair grows out, the cuticle layer starts to unravel and the outside (cuticle layer) starts to get damaged. So, it can work its way up the hair shaft.

The structure of hair is really important to understand. Again, most haircoloring process, such as Permanent color takes place inside the cortex – Temporary and Semi-permanent color adheres to the outside of the hair (cuticle), and Demi-color works on both cuticle & cortex layers, which we will discuss all this later.

Manufacturers Make Haircolor to Work Best on:

Average Texture

and

Normal Porosity

(something we rarely work on)

Most haircolor manufacturers make haircolor to work best on average texture and normal porosity, which is something on which we rarely work.

So, what does that mean? Well, all haircolor manufacturers have a target customer for whom they make the haircolor. That target customer is a person with **average texture** and **normal porosity**.

Let's think about texture for a second.

Texture is the diameter of a hair shaft. Texture is the actual diameter, which will be discussed later.

Average texture is medium diameter. If somebody has very coarse hair, that's not average. If somebody has very fine hair, very skinny hair, that's not average.

So, if we are working with coarse hair, color may need to be left on longer. Or, if the hair is very fine, the color may need to be left on less time. So, the product needs to be altered to make it work.

This also applies to porosity. Some people have very porous hair. This means it is very dry, brittle, and damaged. Some people have very resistant hair. The cuticle on resistant hair is very tight to the hair shaft. This is a condition where the cuticle layer is so tight that the color can't penetrate it. So, we have to do something to make that cuticle layer swell up a little bit, so our haircolor could penetrate it.

So for anybody who doesn't fall into the category of average texture and normal porosity that the manufacturers target, the product will need to be altered.

And the way we alter it is with our **timing and/or developer strength** to make the product work. Otherwise, manufacturers would have to make a color line for people with fine hair, another color line for people with coarse hair, another color line for people with damaged hair. Etc. Manufacturers can't do that and we can't carry all those products, even if the manufacturers made them.

The Secrets of Texture

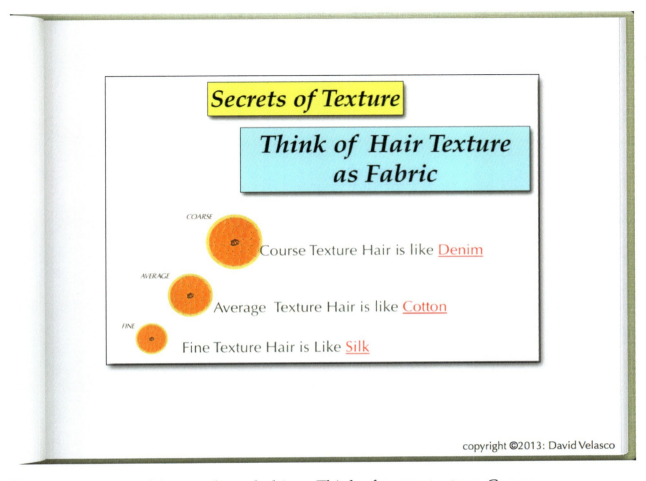

Think of texture as fabric such as clothing. Think of coarse texture. Coarse hair is much thicker with a bigger diameter. Finer hair has a very small diameter; and average hair is a medium diameter.

Think of coarse hair as denim. Denim is like jeans, very coarse, very heavy, and very strong.

Think of fine hair as silk, very fine, very fragile.

Think of average texture as cotton. And if you think of cotton, such as cotton pants. Cotton pants can be washed a number of times.

It used to be, when someone bought jeans, the jeans didn't come prewashed, like they do now. They came strong and stiff. To make them more pliable, they would need to be washed 20 or 30 times. The more denim is washed, the better it is, the softer it gets, the more pliable it gets, and the easier it is to work with.

So, denim can take hundreds of washings and still be great.

The other end of the spectrum, silk, we can't put silk into a washing machine, not even once, because it will completely shred apart. Cotton can be washed many times.

Hair works the same way. If the hair is fine textured, it can't take strong products. The products can't be left on as long. Very gentle products must be used taking very gentle care with them. , For example, when bleaching the hair, instead of using 20-volume developer, you may use a 5-volume or 10-volume developer.

On the other side of the spectrum, coarse hair may need 25- or 30-volume developer to make that bleach or color lift.

So, texture plays a huge role. Understanding the true roles of **Texture and Porosity** is one of the major keys in understanding how haircolor works.

Understanding Texture

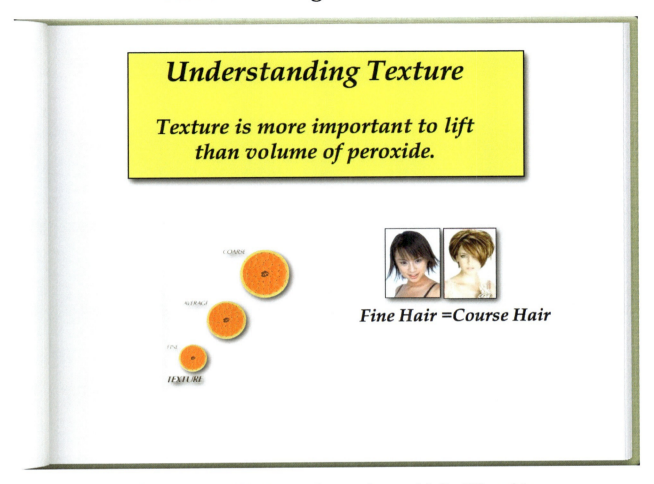

Understanding Texture

Texture is more important to lift than volume of peroxide.

Fine Hair =Course Hair

"Texture is more important to lift than volume of peroxide"...What this means is that a lot of people think using a 30-volume peroxide is going to be able to lift the hair a lot more than using 20-volume peroxide. That's not necessarily the case.

What plays a bigger role is the texture of the hair. This illustration of 2 girls above demonstrates this. The girl on the left-hand side has very fine, skimpy, limp hair. The girl on the right has very thick, coarse hair.

Using the same color or bleach product on both girls - the girl on the left's hair will react much faster to the haircolor than the girl on the right because of the texture. So, for example, when lightening hair, it will make the color go lighter faster and lighter than the coarse hair. In going darker, it will go darker, and go darker faster than the coarse hair. Finer hair will always move much faster with any chemical process, whether it is haircolor, a permanent wave, or chemical relaxer. Fine hair will always react much quicker and much more extreme than coarse-textured hair. Coarse-textured hair will always react slower and not as extreme.

Understanding Porosity

Very Resistant Hair

Average Hair

Very Porous Hair

Damaged Hair

Cement Like Substance

Haircolor Secret
*Porosity can make a Temporary Color Permanent
and a Permanent Color Temporary*

Porosity – a word heard repeatedly. But what does porosity really mean? What does porous hair really mean? What does it look like, in reality?

Above are some illustrations. First of all, let's look at average hair in the top center of the photo. You can see the hair strand. You can see the cuticle layer is slightly raised, but it is not really swollen. It's slightly up. That's average texture.

At the upper left of the photo is very resistant hair. The ripples are hardly visible, where the actual layers are, because the cuticle layer is so tight to the hair.

At the upper right is very porous hair. The hair is tied in a knot. The cuticle layer is porous. It's rising up too much from the hair.

At the lower left is damaged hair, where chunks of the cuticle are completely gone. That is exposing the inside, the cortex of the hair, making hair more susceptible to damaged.

And on the lower right is an illustration of the fibrous bundles inside, where it says **"cement-like substance."** Remember the analogy earlier of a tree? The tree has sap. The hair itself doesn't have sap, per se, but the fibrous bundles are held together with what scientists call a cement-like substance or amorphous glue.

It is not really oozy, like sap. This is not going to be seen or felt in hair. But there is a substance that holds itself together. Going back to the tree analogy, the hair must be kept in the best condition possible, keeping that cortex in good condition to keep the inside of that hair – or sap – from drying out.

Haircolor Secret

Porosity can make a temporary color permanent and a permanent color temporary.

Porosity can make a temporary color permanent and a permanent color temporary…what does that mean?

If you put temporary haircolor on damaged hair, it will go deep into the hair shaft (cortex of the hair) and become like permanent color.

Roux Fanciful® Rinses are temporary haircolor. On good, healthy, virgin hair, they will stain the hair. They don't completely change the color, but will stain the hair for a while. And when shampooed, they will wash completely out. But if you put them on bleached hair, they will make it permanent. They will make a temporary haircolor permanent based on the porosity factor of bleached hair. But this permanent color will not look good, it will look drab and usually ashen.

And by the same token, if somebody has really resistant hair, you can mix permanent haircolor with 20-volume peroxide, leave it on for 30 minutes and you may still see some gray hair when your done.

That is because the hair is too resistant. This is when we get into things like pre-softening.

(We discuss pre-softening in **Volume 3** *Great Gray Coverage.*)

The Natural Level

The starting point of all haircolor processes require finding the natural level. The natural level means the degree of lightness to darkness, minus the tone.

Therefore, talking about a person's natural level is not asking if she is a redhead, blonde or a brunette. That doesn't matter. What is the lightness, or the darkness, minus the tone? She could have red hair, but she could be a level 5, 6 or 7.

This natural level simply means going from dark to very, very light, the natural levels, but there's no tonality to it as in this illustration. It's not appropriate to say, "She's got medium-brown hair," or "She has red hair." The tonality is completely taken out of it. One way to think of it is, for example, like having a glass of Coca-Cola in one hand and a glass of water in the other hand. The Coke can look like a level one, almost black. As the water is poured into that Coke, it gets lighter and lighter. That is what hair level looks like as the levels go lighter.

The problem comes in when people start doing haircolor. They think that when they start lightening somebody's hair, it's going to look like this illustration as they lighten up the hair. And that's not what happens at all, because a lot of red and gold come in the picture. Which we'll discuss soon.

So the starting point for all haircolor formulations is to know what a client's natural level is first, then from that point we will decide what color she wants to be and what we have to do to get us there.

Understanding Natural Pigment

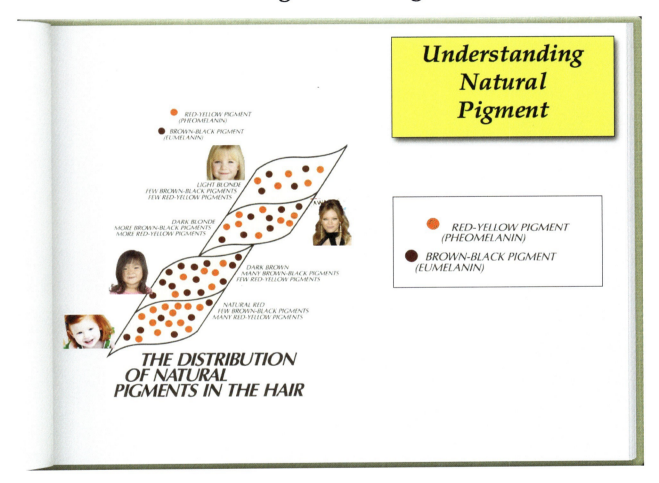

Now let's talk about natural pigmentation. This is what makes somebody a natural redhead, a natural brunette, a natural blonde.

Natural haircolor is made up of a protein called melanin. Melanin is the same protein that gives our eyes and our skin color.

There are 2 types of melanin. One is called pheomelanin pronounced, Fay-O-melanin. This is the red and yellow pigmentation, and the other one is called eumelanin, It starts with E, but it's pronounced U-melanin. This is the one that give us brown/black pigmentation.

This illustration shows the distribution of natural pigmentation, just to give a general idea. The little girl at top left is a natural blonde. Light blonde hair has very few brown and black pigments, and very few red and yellow pigments. So, there's not a whole lot of strong pigmentation in her hair at all.

As this person gets older, a lot of times, their haircolor will become a little darker. She becomes a dark blonde like the person on the right of the photo. A dark blonde has more brown and black pigments and more red and yellow pigments, but none of them are dominant. They just increase a bit more in depth but none are very dominant.

The young Asian girl illustrates a more ethnic type situation. She has many of the brown and black pigmentation and few of the red/yellow pigmentation. She has a lot of eumelanin and very few pheomelanin.

The little girl at the bottom is a natural redhead; she has a very strong red color. She has very few eumelanin and a lot more pheomelanin, and a lot more strong red. Red is a very dominant color.

A lot of times, that's hereditary. If your Mother or Father is a redhead, chances are you are going to be a redhead. When there's a redhead in the family, it's a very strong gene or dominant gene that goes through the family a lot of times. That is how the distribution of natural pigment works out.

Understanding the Decolorization of

Natural Pigment

Many times a client with Medium to Dark Brown hair will sit in our chair and say something like this, *"You know, I don't want to be a blonde, I really don't want to be a blonde, but I just want my hair to be a few shades lighter", but I don't want to see any red."*

That's impossible to do. It is important to be able to explain to them why it's impossible, because they think the hair goes from dark brown to light brown like the Coca-Cola analogy I gave you earlier. They think that's how it happens. And also, a lot of hairdressers think that too, and that's why they ruin a lot of hair. That's not how it works at all.

When you began to lighten natural haircolor it goes through what is known as "shades of lift" which means that instead of going from dark brown, to dark blonde, to medium blonde, to light blonde it goes from Brown to reddish-brown to red, to orange, to gold, to yellow and to pale yellow.

On the next page you will see the Contributing Color Pigment Chart and learn exactly what you could expect to see as you lighten someone's hair.

30

Contributing Color Pigment Chart

CONTRIBUTING COLOR PIGMENT CHART		
NATURAL HAIRCOLOR	LEVEL	CONTRIBUTING COLOR PIGMENT
LIGHTEST BLONDE	10	PALE YELLOW →
VERY LIGHT BLONDE	9	YELLOW →
LIGHT BLONDE	8	DARK YELLOW →
MEDIUM BLONDE	7	GOLD →
DARK BLONDE	6	GOLD ORANGE →
LIGHT BROWN	5	ORANGE →
MEDIUM BROWN	4	RED ORANGE →
DARK BROWN	3	DARK RED ORANGE →
VERY DARK BROWN	2	RED BROWN →
BLACK	1	DARK RED BROWN →

This chart is what is known as the contributing color pigment chart.

The words "contributing color pigment" is one of many names that people call this in the hairdressing world. Some people say it's the underlying pigment. Some people say it's the contributing color pigment. Some people say residual color value. There are all kinds of different names. Which is kind of confusing.

Looking at the chart you will see, down the middle is the levels, level 1-10, level one being like black, level 10 being the lightest blonde. On the left-hand side are the natural haircolor levels. This is like the natural level colors showed earlier. And the right-hand column shows you what to expect as the hair is lightened.

So, for example, if we were lightening a level 3 client, who is dark brown, when it is lightened, a Dark Red-Orange is achieved. Even if it's a level 6, which is pretty light, when lightening a level 6, it will be a strong Gold-Orange.

If your were doing a bleach-out, as in doing a double process blonde, many times you will be fooled because when the product (bleach) is on the hair, the product is either going to be white or it's going to have a blue cast to it.

So, when the hair is checked, scraping a little bit of bleach off to see if it's light enough, the white bleach or the blue bleach can diffuse the yellow, conceal the yellow a little bit, so it can't be determined how yellow it really is until washed out. When it is washed out and dried, a hairdresser might say, "Oh my gosh, she's so yellow! What happened now?"

If that happens, the only way to fix that is to go back in and re-bleach again. The bleach needs mixed again and reapplied.

Especially when first starting out in this business, it can be confusing. It happened to me, even, after being very experienced."

Every time hair is lightened, it goes through these shades of lift, and the warm tones will always be exposed.

Key#2 -- Secret of the Products

Key Point Number #2 is the **"Secret of the Products."**

Now, that we have a thorough understanding of hair and texture and porosity. Let's talk about the products and what they are, exactly.

4 Main Types of Haircolor

4 Main Types of Haircolor

1. *Temporary Haircolor*
2. *Semi-Permanent Haircolor*
3. *Demi Haircolor*
4. *Permanent Haircolor.*

copyright ©2013: David Velasco

There are 4 main types of haircolor which are:

1) Temporary haircolor

2) Semi-permanent haircolor

3) Demi-permanent haircolor

4) Permanent haircolor.

In the world of haircolor it is important to understand when and why to use a certain type of haircolor.

Where Haircolor Lives

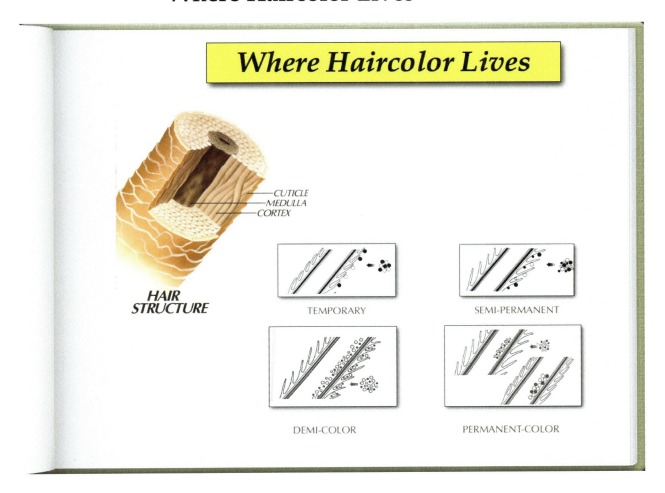

In this illustration are 4 squares. Each one shows you exactly where the haircolor molecules live inside the hair.

In the next few pages we will look at these in detail, but for now I just want you to realize that even though there are 4 types of haircolor available to us, chances are you only carry 2 of the 4 in your salon, demi & permanent haircolor.

The reason is that the other 2, temporary and semi-permanent haircolor, are mainly used as home haircolor and sold at drug stores and grocery stores. (Although not always)

Temporary Haircolor

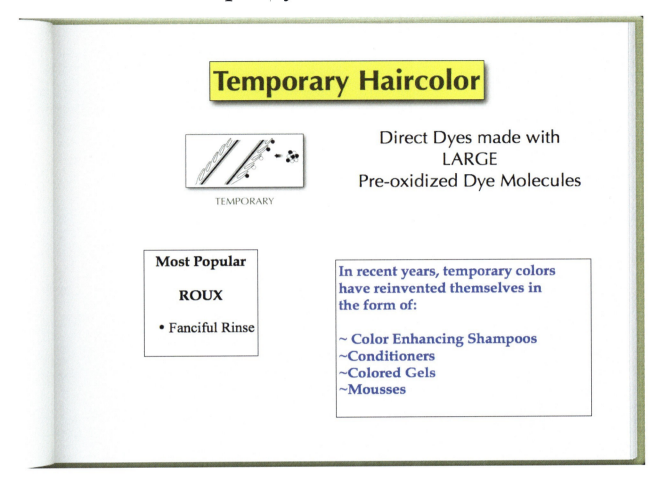

The first one we'll look at is called temporary haircolor. Think about Roux Fanciful® Rinses, and there are others. Color-enhancing shampoos, conditioners, color-enhancing gels and mousses that have color in them - these are all forms of temporary haircolor.

They're made with what's called **pre-oxidized dye molecules**. In other words, they're not made with oxidative dye molecules; they're made with dye molecules that have already been oxidized, like in the laboratory or in the manufacturing plant. Thus you do not need to mix them with any kind of developer.

Temporary color has very large, pre-oxidized dye molecules. So when you apply it, the large dye molecules stick to the outer layer (cuticle) of the hair.

In the illustration you can see the little ridges of the cuticle layer. The dye molecules for the temporary color are very large. Think of them as very large balls. They can only kind of stick onto the outer layer of the hair.

Assuming the hair's in good condition, after one shampoo it's going to be washed away completely. If the hair has been pre-bleached, or if the hair has been damaged in any way, like chemical relaxer or permanent wave, the cuticle layer has been lifted up or, in some cases torn away, temporary haircolor will go deeper into the hair shaft (cortex) and it will stain hair and not come out at all.

Years ago, when I had a salon in New York, I had 2 clients who were both flight attendants, and they were roommates, one was a heavily-highlighted, blonde, with bleached highlights, The other one had her hair colored red.

At that time, I sold a line of color-enhancing shampoos and conditioners. So, the blonde bought one for a blonde hair and the redhead bought one for redheads.

Well, one day, while the blonde was taking a shower in their apartment, she saw the redhead's products there, shampoos and conditioners, and she thought, *"Hey, that's like temporary color. It might be kind of cool to be a redhead for the day."* She thought it would be fun. So, she uses her roommate's products, the Red shampoo and the conditioner, on her hair.

When she finished and looked at her hair she freaked out.

She thought her hair would be a beautiful red color like her roommates but instead she looked like Ronald McDonald, a horrible, ugly red color. It was great for the redhead to keep her hair red. But when put on bleached hair, it looks totally different.

Now, she washes her hair 5 or 6 times, to try to get this out, but it would not come out.

So, she comes back to me in tears. I had to do a major color correction on her. The only way to get her back to blonde was to bleach it back out.

Semi-Permanent Haircolor

Semi-Permanent Haircolor

SEMI-PERMANENT

Direct Dyes made with
LARGE & SMALL
Pre-oxidized Dye Molecules

Haircolor Secret

A semi-permanent color is a lotion type product that is poured straight out of the bottle onto the hair.

It is never mixed with anything else.

NO: powders, crystals, tablets, developers or lotions of any kind

It's important to understand is that there is a difference between **semi-permanent color and demi-permanent color**. A lot of people don't understand the difference, and a lot of product manufacturers have confused the issue because many times they bunch them together, and they should not be bunched together.

Semi-permanent haircolor has 2 types of dye molecules, the **large pre-oxidized dye molecules**, like temporary color, and it also has **small pre-oxidized dye molecules** and no developer is used with it. A true semi-permanent color is like a lotion-type product that is poured out of the bottle, straight onto the hair.

Examples of a true semi-permanent color would be the Clairol Beautiful Series, like Beautiful Browns, Beautiful Reds and Beautiful Blondes. These products are very popular in the ethnic community, who work on African-American hair, because so many times African-American clients have hair that's been chemically relaxed. As a result the hair is very, fragile. And because of the porosity factor, you don't have to use peroxide. So, they can use a semi-permanent color and get really nice colors out of it. *(For more information on coloring African-American hair see* **Volume 9** *in this series: Coloring Natural and Chemically relaxed African-American hair)*

Now, because of the fact that semi-permanent color has large pre-oxidized dye molecules and very small pre-oxidized dye molecules, there is better penetration of color in the hair than temporary color.

What happens with this, typically, is the lotion is put on the hair, a plastic bag is put on their hair and they sit under the dryer for 15 or 20 minutes. The dryer swells the cuticle layer slightly, and allows those little tiny dye molecules to penetrate under the cuticle layer a little bit. It still does not have the ability to go into the cortex, but it lodges into the cuticle layer. Therefore, when the hair is washed, the color doesn't wash right out.

Years ago, these colors were called 6-week rinses. This was because years ago, ladies just washed their hair once a week. Before the shampoo and blow-drying era, ladies would go to the hair salon or beauty parlors and have their hair done once a week. They would get a semi-permanent color, and it would last about 6 shampoos, that's why they called them 6-week rinses.

But now, people wash their hair every day. Some people wash their hair twice a day. For example, if they are going to the gym or working out, they may wash their hair twice a day. So, again, these rinses wash out very quickly. And that's why they're not so popular as an in-salon service unless you are working primarily on an African-America clientele.

Keep in mind that semi-permanent colors adhere to the outer layer of the hair. They still do not have the ability to go into the cortex of the hair (unless the hair has been pre-lightened or is very porous). And the reason for that is because there's no catalyst. It is not mixed with any kind of lotion or peroxide. It goes straight out of the bottle into the hair.

Demi-Haircolor

Demi-Haircolor

DEMI-COLOR

Direct Dyes made with
LARGE & SMALL
Pre-oxidized Dye Molecules
and
Molecules in need of
Oxidization

Haircolor Secret

Demi- Haircolor is an oxidative tint, it is always mixed with a catalyst of some kind which starts the oxidation process

The Catalyst is usually hydrogen peroxide but could be: powders, crystals, tablets (dehydrated ammonia compounds)

The third category is Demi-color.

Demi-colors have only been around for about 20 years but they have emerged as one of our industries leading types of color. This is primarily because of the many ways they can be used.

Demi-colors are very popular because they don't change the hair dramatically, so they're great for using on men, for example, because men don't want a dramatic color change. They're great on women, especially some one who's never had color before, since they are being introduced to color. It's not so dramatic.

Demi-colors are completely different than both, Semi-permanent & Permanent haircolor in that they are actually made with two different types of dye molecules.

Demi color is made with the same large and small dye molecules (Known as direct dyes) like we have in semi-permanent color, but it also has dye molecules in need of oxidation, just like permanent haircolor. That is why you must always use a developer with demi- haircolor. (Temporary and semi-permanent haircolors never use any type of developer)

It's this unique duel pigmenting system that gives demi-color its advantage over semi-permanent color, when it comes to gray coverage. Also because the developer is usually very weak, demi-colors will not lift the natural color and thus not create unwanted warm tones like permanent color can.

Demi-color has a combination of both dye molecules. It has the dye molecules of a semi-permanent color, that adheres to the outer layer of the hair, and it also has some of the dye molecules similar to permanent color, that actually penetrate the hair shaft, and goes slightly into the cortex of the hair. Although, like this illustration shows, it does not go as deeply into the cortex as permanent color does. It does go into the cortex a little.

Demi-color does what is called: **"fades on tone."**

So, for example, if someone is a brunette and using permanent haircolor , when the color starts to fade, a lot of times the hair will start to look red. The brunettes will turn red. That's because all permanent color works on the premise that it has to pre-lighten the natural color first, before it injects the artificial color into the hair.

Demi-color doesn't pre-lighten the hair at all. Demi-color is what is known as a **progressive tint**, which means it can only go progressively darker (not lighter).

Demi-color will fade, but it will fade on tone. That brunette won't go from brown to red; she will go from brown to a lighter shade of brown because there was no lifting action in the coloring process.

What really fades on the demi colors are the large and small dye molecules that only adhere to the cuticle layer of the hair, just like semi-permanent color, and the ones that penetrate the hair shaft, like permanent color, stay there.

So, if someone's hair is colored with demi-color, even if she has gray hair, she will get good coverage and a line of demarcation. It has structurally changed the color of the hair, but not as strong or as permanently as permanent color.

Traditionally, 20-volume peroxide is used with permanent color, On some occasions, 10 or 30 may be used, but traditionally 20-volume peroxide is used. Demi-colors use about 5-10-volume peroxide.

Volume 2 *How Haircolor Really Works* covers my top 10 list for ways to use demi-color.

Permanent Haircolor

Permanent Haircolor

PERMANENT-COLOR

Made with
100% Oxidative Dyes

Haircolor Secret

*Permanent haircolor is made with "Oxidative Dyes".
These are dyes that change their molecular structure when
mixed with a catalyst (hydrogen peroxided)*

All Permanent haircolors have dye molecules that have to be oxidized. In other words, they have to have a catalyst that is usually hydrogen peroxide. Also all permanent haircolor must have ammonia, the lighter the shade, the higher the ammonia content in the tube.

The ammonia in the color and the hydrogen peroxide together create a series of combustion gasses. These gases create a few things that happen simultaneously.

When you mix the developer (peroxide) with the color, the dye molecules start to grow. In other words, peroxide is H_2O_2. It's hydrogenated water. It's water with oxygen.

When that oxygen comes together with the dye molecules and ammonia, it infuses oxygen into the dye molecules and makes the tiny, tiny dye molecules start to grow.

Also, when the 2 are mixed together, it creates 2 different kinds of gasses. One is known as **"Free Ammonia",** that's the strong ammonia smell that you smell as you are mixing the color. The other is called **"Bound Ammonia"**

Free ammonia is a strong gas that kick-starts the oxidation process. And, at the same time, it also kick-starts the swelling of the cuticle layer of the hair and the decolorizing of the natural pigment of the hair, The cuticle layer of hair has to swell some to allow those dye molecules to penetrate into the cortex of the hair.

After a few minutes goes by, that strong ammonia smell will dissipate and calm down. That's when the bound ammonia takes over. The job of the bound ammonia is to continue with the oxidation process throughout the length of the color processing time, usually 30 to 45 minutes, after which time the color will be too weak to do anything else.

Here is a simplified summary of the oxidation process.

What happens, in essence, is that color goes on the hair, the cuticle layer starts to swell, the tiny dye artificial molecules penetrate into the cuticle layer of the hair, and at the same time it begins to decolorize the natural haircolor pigment.

When the dye molecules are in the cortex they start to grow. They get bigger, and fatter, until finally they get so fat that they can't come out of the same hole they went into.

Imagine they're all so fat, and they're all holding hands. And now, the process is over 30 minutes later. The hair is shampooed, and the residual color that's on the outside of the hair comes out, but the color that's penetrated into the hair shaft stays in there permanently.

The Secret of when to use a Demi-color _vs._ Permanent color:

Use a _Demi- color_ any time you want to:
- Stay the same level
- Go darker
- Stay the same level and change the tone.

Use a _Permanent color_ any time you want to go lighter or brighter.

So when should you use a demi color instead of a permanent color or visa/versa?

As a general rule, use a demi-color anytime you want to stay the same level and just blend in gray, you want to stay the same level and change the tone slightly (i.e.: add some red to brown or blonde), or if you want to go darker. (Going darker needs no lift.) In those 3 situations, a permanent color probably isn't needed.

Use a permanent color anytime you want to go lighter or brighter or have very resistant gray hair. In other words, if you want to make somebody's hair lighter (blonder), or if you want to make somebody a brighter redhead, you've got to lighten up the hair and the way to do that is to use permanent color. Demi-color is not strong enough for the challenges of lightening or brightening, Remember, demi-colors are deposit-only haircolors. They can only deposit; they can't lift.

Key #3 -- The Secret of Formulation

The 2 Variables of Timing and Developer Strength

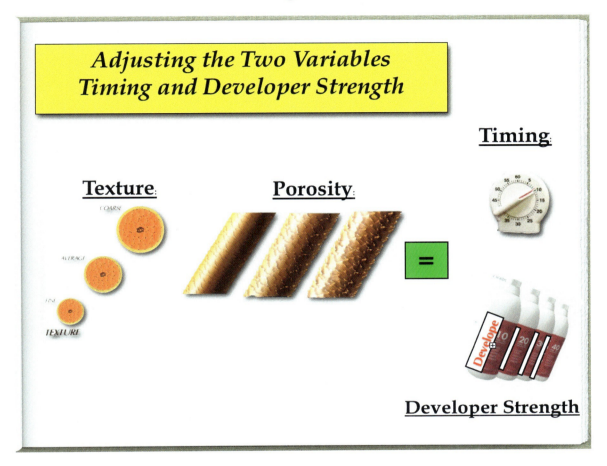

Because manufacturers make haircolor to work best on **normal texture and average porosity**, as we discussed earlier, as colorists, we have to be able to alter the product, to bend the product to work for us to use on hair that may not be average texture or normal porosity. And we do that by understanding texture and porosity (which we discussed earlier) and by using that information to **adjust our timing and/or developer strength.**

<u>Timing:</u>

- By leaving the color on longer, we can get better penetration and better gray coverage.

- By leaving the color on less time, we will get less penetration and a more subtle color result.

Developer Strength:

- By increasing the strength of the developer, we are able to achieve higher lifting action and faster lightening.

- By using a lower strength developer we will get less depositing action and slower lifting action.

Understanding Levels and Tones

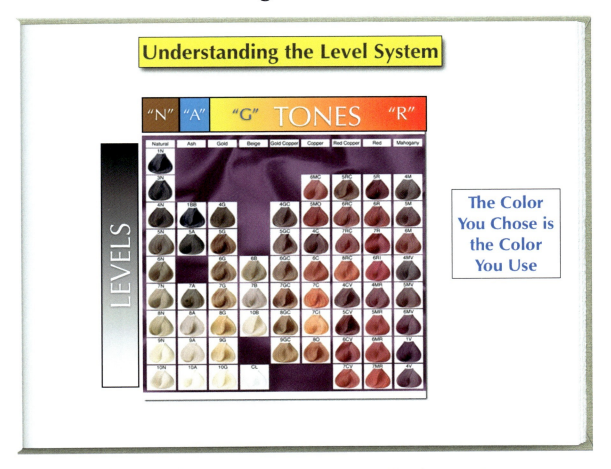

Years ago, when formulating haircolor, there was no level system in America. We used a system called the "Shades of Lift System," where a mathematical equation had to be worked out to decide what color to use.

With the Level System, which came from Europe during the 1970's, you choose the color you want from the swatch book and you use that color. You alter it by changing the developer strength or the timing.

Of course, this sounds easier than it actually is because we have to play within the rules of haircolor by using the contributing color pigment chart, taking into account the hair's texture and porously and the limitations of the tint we are using.

Generally speaking though, when reading a swatch chart, the first row, will usually be the N series, N stands for natural or neutral. It all depends on what product line is being used. Some haircolor manufacturers call it natural and some call it neutral, but it means the same thing.

Levels go from level 1 to level 10, level 1 being black and level 10 being lightest blonde. Think of this color base just like the natural haircolor levels we spoke about earlier as in, lightness to darkness, minus the tone.

That's the level (light-dark). That's not the tone (color).

When we talk about tones, we can go across the top of the chart. The example chart in the illustration has ash, gold, beige, copper, copper-red, and mahogany. These are different tones of color.

So, you can have all different tones of colors in different levels.

The only one that's different is the N series, which I consider it to be a brown base color. And the best way to think of it is by using the Coca-Cola analogy that I gave you earlier.

Now, the N series is made primarily to be intermixed with the other colors. For example, if you're making somebody a redhead, putting a straight red color on someone with gray or a lighter natural color may be too vibrant. So we would use an N series brown base color in the same level to mix into the red color to mellow out the red a little bit. (In **Volume 2** *How Haircolor Really Works* you will learn about mixing ratios to achieve different color results.)

Now, the N series, if used by itself, is a little bit flat.

If somebody has 75%-100% gray/white hair and a straight N series color is applied, the hair may look a little flat. It will cover the gray and it may be acceptable, but it's not going to be warm and it will not have any luster to it. It's going to be kind of a flat, boring tone.

2 Different Tonal Systems

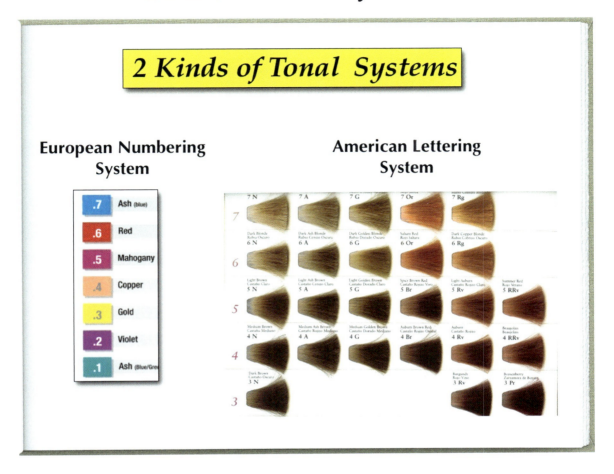

Just to make haircolor a little more confusing, you need to understand that there are 2 different tonal systems. There's the European numbering system. The European color lines use the level number and then a dot (.).1, .2, .3. or stroke sign (/)/4,/5,/6 before the tone. The second system is the one used by American haircolor manufacturers which is a number and lettering system, like 7Rg, which stands for level 7-red-gold base or 8Rv, which stands for level 8 with a red-violet base.

Till this day many haircolor manufacturers will put both the numbers and the letters on a tube, bottle or box of color. But the European numbering system is dominant in our industry because most (not all) color lines come from Europe.

However, even within the European numbering system you **will find that different companies will label their tones with different numbers**. So make sure that you study your manufacturer's literature to learn its system for labeling its particular haircolor line.

This is also why for the purposes of this book, and all the rest of the books in this course, I will always use the American Lettering System to explain haircolor formulations, because they will always be constant.

Color Identification

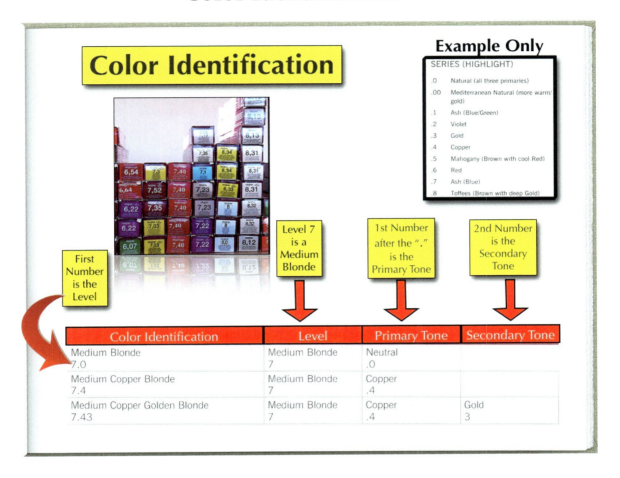

The number on the box or tube is called the color identification. The first number seen before the stroke or dot is always going to be the level of the color. Then after the stroke or dot will be the number indicating the primary tone in the tube and then a second number indicating the secondary tone in the tube.

In the example in the illustration, you will see that the level of the color is 7, with a primary color tone of 4, which in this example is copper, and a secondary color tone of 3, which is gold. That's how it's read.

Understanding Developers

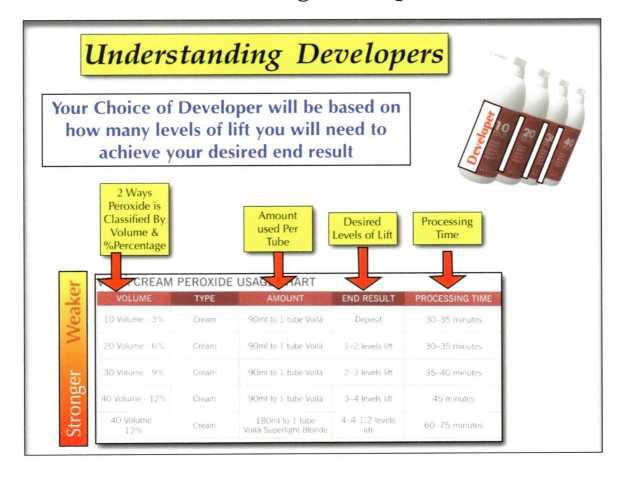

Choosing developers will be based on how many levels of lift will be needed to achieve the desired end result.

Basically, developers run from weak to stronger, 10-volume, 20-volume, 30-volume, 40-volume. Sometimes, developers will appear in percentage: 3%, 6%, 9%, 12%. Some manufacturers will display it both ways.

Again, this is partially because of the American and European influences. Americans companies will usually use volume, and the Europeans will usually use percentage.

<u>KEY:</u>

10 Volume = 3%

20 Volume = 6%

30 Volume = 9%

40 Volume = 12%

In the USA we rarely use anything stronger than 40 Volume developers, but in the rest of the world 60, 80 & 100 Volumes are commonly used (especially for off-the-scalp work such as highlighting).

When to Use Which Developer

So here's the key as to when to use what developer when formulating your haircolor.

10-Volume

10-Voloume is a good choice if working on very fine or very fragile hair. In my book on coloring African-American hair (**Volume 9** of this course) we give you many haircolor formulations using 10-volume developer because many times African-American hair can be very fragile, especially if it has been chemically processed.

Also you may use 10-Volume developer if you are looking for a vary subtle change as in just trying to lighten the base slightly or to add some tone as in replenishing a faded color.

I also always use 10-Volume, when I want gentle slow moving bleach.

20-Volume

In the vast majority of work you will be using 20-volume developer. Anytime you want to lift 1 to 2 levels, as in taking someone from a level 5 to a level 7, 20-volume is the choice.

And if you follow what I teach, you will almost never try to lift someone more than two levels during a single process application, because you will be exposing way too much of the contributing color pigment and the hair will look too warm (red or gold). You'll learn more about that in **Volume 2,** *How Haircolor Really Works.*

You will also use 20-volume, if you want to stay the same level as in just covering gray hair or even if you want to go darker. Although for this I would probably opt for demi-color, unless the client has very stubborn/resistant gray to cover.

30-Volume

Use 30-volume anytime you want to lift between 3 to 4 levels, as in making a blonde, brighter redhead or in a highlighting situation.

40-Volume

Use 40-volume anytime you want to lift 4 to 5 levels. As in using the color of a highlighting service. Also 40 Volume is used many times for high lifting blonde shades which are also discussed in volume 2 of this course.

Secrets of the Color Wheel

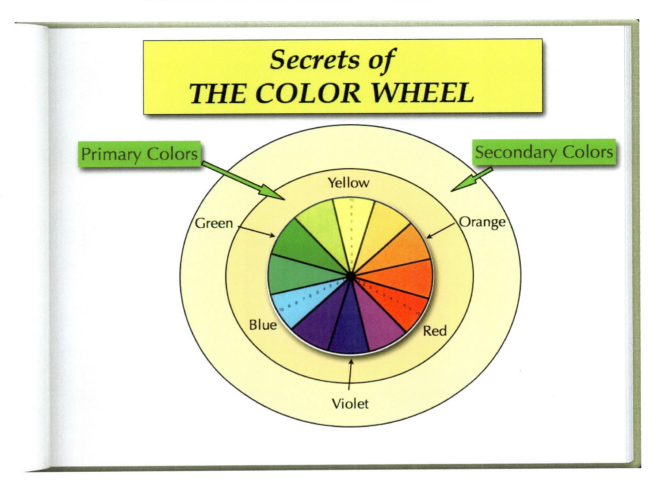

In beauty school we all learned about the color wheel. To tell you the truth, that is about the only thing that beauty school taught me about haircolor…*and it was wrong*.

For example, I was taught that if a client's hair is green (because of bad haircolor, not because she wanted it that way), I could go to the opposite side of the color wheel (which is red) and use that color to neutralize the green.

Once you have been doing haircolor as long as me, you realize that this does not work. If a client's hair has turned green, due to poor color choice or overly porous hair, you must completely remove the green color first with a mild bleach solution. Once the green is out of the hair, you can recolor it to the color you would like it to be. So the whole naturalization thing does not work the way we were taught. (This is discussed in detail in other books in this course.)

However, we can learn some other things about haircolor by looking at the color wheel. The color wheel can be divided in half – there is the warm side, yellow, orange, red. Any color between yellow and red and all the orange colors are the warm base colors.

And on the cool side of the color wheel are blue, green and violet.

What is interesting is that there's only one primary cool color - blue and 2 primary warm colors – red and yellow. But anytime blue is mixed with either one of the other 2 warm colors, the new color produced will always be a cool color.

Example:

Blue & Yellow – become Green (a cool color)

Blue & Red – become Violet (a cool color)

This is because blue is the strongest and most dominate color in the universe.

Also when these colors are mixed, as I did in the example, you will be making what is known as a "secondary color" or a second generation of color.

All of this will start to make more since in the next section when we discuss tones and basses.

#4 – Secrets of Application & Timing

So How Do We Do It?

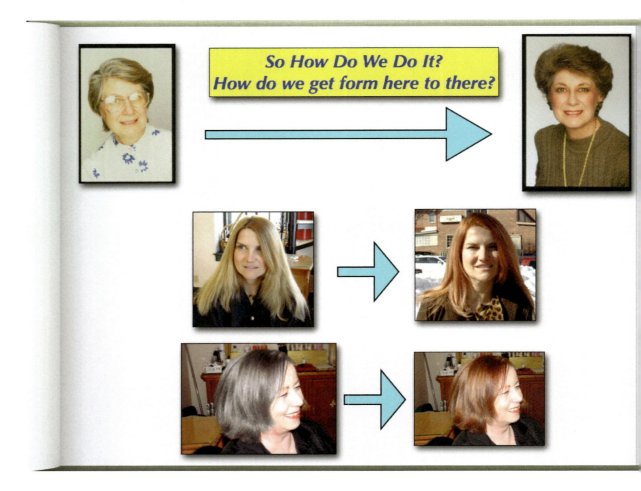

How do we get from here to there? How do we take a client who looks like the woman on the left and make her look like the photos on the right?

Well, in this section I am going to give you an overview of the haircoloring procedure by showing you my thought process behind my color choices. This will give you an idea of what to do. However, in this book we can only scratch the surface of haircolor formulation and in **Volume 2** – *How Haircolor Really Works* we will go indepth of exactly how to formulate haircolor.

It All Starts With the Consultation

It all Starts with the Consultation

Haircolor Consultation Checklist

- What is the overall condition of the hair?
- What is the hair's density?
- What is the hair's texture?
- What is the hair's formation?
- What is a hair's porosity?
- What is the hair's natural level?
- What is the hair's percentage of gray/white?
- What is the hair's natural tone?
- What is the agreed upon new color?
- What is the gentlest product that can be used to achieve the desired results?
- What is the plan and formula?
- What is the application technique?
- What is the timing?
- What kind of maintenance will be needed?
- What home hair care products will be needed?
- What will the cost be?

It all starts with the haircolor consultation. This is where you will assess the characteristics of her hair (condition, porosity, natural level, percentage of gray, etc.) and discusses what color she would like to be, as well as what you may recommend to her.

There actually is a lot more information that you will need to be obtaining during the haircolor consultation, but for now let's just stay with the hair itself. For more information on haircolor consultations see **Volume 10** – *Haircolor Consultation Skills* in this course.

Below I have given you a checklist of points to consider during the haircolor consultation. This list might look long and confusing to you now, but soon it will all become second nature as you work through this course.

Haircolor Formulation Checklist

Foremost, make sure you covered all your bases before applying the color to the hair by using the following checklist to help you stay organized:

- ☑ What is the overall condition of the hair?
- ☑ What is the hair's density?
- ☑ What is the hair's texture?
- ☑ What is the hair's formation?
- ☑ What is a hair's porosity?
- ☑ What is the hair's natural level?
- ☑ What is the hair's percentage of gray/white?
- ☑ What is the hair's natural tone?
- ☑ What is agreed upon regarding new color?
- ☑ What is the gentlest product that can be used to achieve the desired results?
- ☑ What is the plan and formula?
- ☑ What is the application technique?
- ☑ What is the timing a developer strength ?
- ☑ What kind of maintenance will be needed?
- ☑ What home hair care products will be needed?
- ☑ What will the cost be?

Mary's Makeover

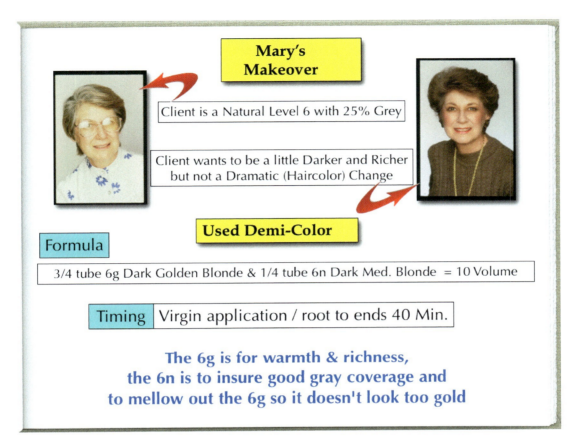

Mary's Makeover

Client is a Natural Level 6 with 25% Grey

Client wants to be a little Darker and Richer but not a Dramatic (Haircolor) Change

Used Demi-Color

Formula

3/4 tube 6g Dark Golden Blonde & 1/4 tube 6n Dark Med. Blonde = 10 Volume

Timing Virgin application / root to ends 40 Min.

The 6g is for warmth & richness,
the 6n is to insure good gray coverage and
to mellow out the 6g so it doesn't look too gold

Mary's Makeover

Mary is in her late 60's and has never had her hair colored before, so she is very apprehensive about coloring her hair. During our consultation she made it very clear to me, that she wants to color her hair, but she does not want it to look fake. Also, she wants to have her hair look richer but not too dark.

Mary only has about 25% gray, but the once brown shiny hair she had when she was younger is now a flat drab brown with no shine or luster to it.

Since Mary really does not want a major haircolor change, but instead only wants to cover or "blend in" the gray, and she also wants a richer medium brown color, I did not see a need to use traditional permanent haircolor, so I opted for a demi color for her.

Her pigmented hair is about a level 6, dual flat brown with about 25% gray. Her texture is medium and her porosity is normal but could be slightly resistant because of the gray that's never been colored before, so for this reason I may have to leave the demi color on a little longer than the normal 30 minutes.

Based on all this information, the formula I used was:

3/4 tube 6g (or 6.3) and 1/4 tube 6n (or 6.0) with the proper demi color developer.

Note: some demi colors come with 2 developers, a weaker one (about 5 Vol.) that is used for toning or replenishing color and a slightly stronger one (about 10 vol) that is used for better gray coverage.

So for Mary I used the stronger one and I left the color on Mary an extra 10 minutes for a total of 40 minutes all together for better coverage on her slightly resistant gray hair.

The end result was a lovely rich warm golden brown with the gray coming out slightly lighter.

Why didn't I use a permanent color?

As I said earlier, Mary had never had any color on her hair. She was very apprehensive about the whole process to start, so I wanted to keep her hair looking as natural as possible. For this reason I did not feel the need to use anything stronger or more permanent than a demi color.

Valerie's Makeover

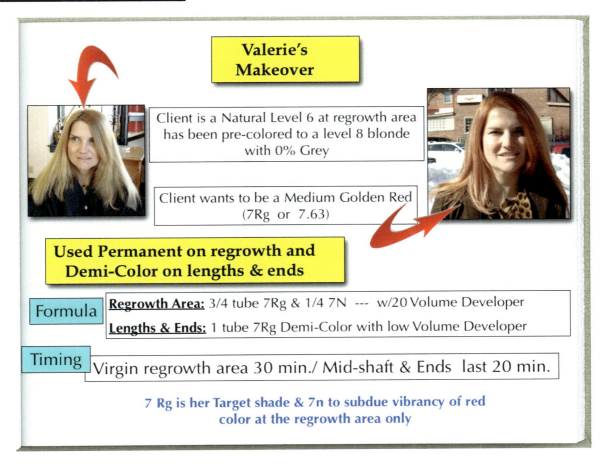

Valerie's Makeover

Client is a Natural Level 6 at regrowth area has been pre-colored to a level 8 blonde with 0% Grey

Client wants to be a Medium Golden Red (7Rg or 7.63)

Used Permanent on regrowth and Demi-Color on lengths & ends

Formula
Regrowth Area: 3/4 tube 7Rg & 1/4 7N --- w/20 Volume Developer
Lengths & Ends: 1 tube 7Rg Demi-Color with low Volume Developer

Timing Virgin regrowth area 30 min./ Mid-shaft & Ends last 20 min.

7 Rg is her Target shade & 7n to subdue vibrancy of red color at the regrowth area only

Valerie's Makeover

Valerie's natural haircolor is about a level 6. She has been coloring her hair for a long time with a permanent color to make it blonder using a level 8 golden blonde.

For this reason her hair is slightly on the porous side but not damaged. Her texture is slightly course and she has very strong hair.

After being blonde for a long time, now she wanted a major change and become a redhead.

Because of the light brown regrowth area (roots), I knew that I would have to use a permanent haircolor to get her lighter and brighter (red). (Remember the rule, to make hair lighter and brighter, use a permanent color.)

However, the rest of her hair had already been lightened with a permanent color to a blonde shade at about a level 8. So for Valerie I had to makeup **two different formulas**, one for the natural regrowth area and a different one for the rest of her hair.

Our target color on which we both agreed during the consultation was a medium red-gold level 7 (7Rg).

In this case I had to lighten the regrowth area from a light brown to a medium red-blonde and darken the blonde hair to the same red-blonde color.

For the regrowth area I used my target shade, ¾ tube 7Rg (level 7 Red- gold base) and ¼ tube 7N with 20 Volume developer. I used ¼ tube of my "N" series so the regrowth area (roots) won't look too bright, then for the rest of her hair, I used 7Rg demi color with the demi's low volume developer.

I used a demi color on the blonde hair, because here I was not lightening. Instead, I was deepening the color so I did not need the extra ammonia that a permanent color would have given me.

In Valerie's example, keep in mind that her blonde hair was only lifted about 2 levels from her natural haircolor (level 6 to a level 8). So there was still a lot of gold in her hair for me to work on top of.

If her hair had been made blonde by use of a very high lifting shade or bleach, as in heavily bleached out highlights, or if it would have been overly porous, I would not have been able to just put a demi color over that. If that had been the case, I would have had to use a demi color first as a filler (using a lighter red-gold shade) and then re-colored again with demi color using my target shade.

Note: In **Volume 2** *How Haircolor Really Works* in this series, we will discuss how to use fillers for tint backs in detail.

Secrets of Making Gray Hair, Red

Ann's Makeover

And then finally we have Ann's makeover; Ann is gray and she wants to be a redhead. That's a little bit more complicated.

What I want to do here is to give you a **"safe"** formula of color ratio to use whenever you are working on someone with gray/white hair.

You see, because the hair is gray/white, the hair will take the full impact of the color. Therefore, if you use a straight red color on this person she will look way too vibrant, as in a screaming redhead. This is very undesirable. So in order to keep that from happening we need to mellow out the color by mixing the red color with a brown base color (neutral, natural or gold).

So this always brings up the question: How much brown base color should I put in the formula verses the red color? Or put another way, what are the color ratios for this client?

So here is how you would do this type of client's color.

The first step is: the hair needs to be analyzed and a decision needs to be made as to how much gray is actually in the hair. Is it 25% or less gray? Is it about 50/50 gray? Or is it 75% gray or more? Even if it's 100% gray, put her in the 75% to 100% gray category.

The second step is: if it's around 25% gray, use 25% of a brown base color. So, in this case, 5N would be the brown base color, and 75% of the desired shade. My desired shade for Ann was 5Rv (Level 5 with a violet base or Light Auburn).

I would use 25% of my brown base color. That way, the gray doesn't get really strong and pungent red. The neutral is going to help subdue some of the red color.

Now, if the hair is around 50/50, use 50% of the brown base color and 50% of the red shade.

If the hair is 75% gray or more, 75% of the formula should be the brown base color and only 25% is the red color. And even though so much brown is being used, versus a little bit of red, she will still have red hair when all finished.

Ann's color (permanent haircolor) was mixed with 20-volume developer, then applied roots to ends and left on for 30 minutes.

Now, after you have finished the color, if it appears too subtle, it can be altered the next time, if necessary, but at least this give you a starting point, what I call a point of reference and a "safe ratio" to start the haircoloring process.

In **Volume 3** of this series *Great Gray Coverage*, you will learn exactly how to make gray hair any color you wish.

**Other Haircolor Education Programs
From David Velasco**

HaircolorTradeSecrets.com

FREE Haircolor Ebook
Haircolor Books - Creative Foiling DVD's - Audio CD's

Trade Secrets of a Haircolor Expert
David Velasco

HaircolorClubhouse.com

FREE Haircolor VIDEOS
Network with Thousands of Hairdressers - Haircolor BLOGS - Haircolor Photos

 **The Haircolor Experts
"Networking Club House"**
by David Velasco

HaircolorUniversity.com

12 Month - MultiMedia E-Course in the Art of Haircolor
Streaming and Downloadable - Videos - Audios - PDF

Haircolor *University* By David Velasco

David Velasco "LIVE" Class DVD's

Available at:

HaircolorTradeSecrets.com

Haircolor Trade Secrets
"LIVE" Class DVD's

- Haircolor 101 – The Beginning
- How Haircolor Really Works
- Gray Coverage Class
- Amazing Redheads Class
- Exotic Brunettes Class
- Single Process Blondes Blondes
- Double Process Blondes
- Color Correction Made Easy
- Color Correction for Redheads
- Color Correction for Blondes
- Color Correction for Gary Coverage
- 101 Haircolor Trade Secrets
- Men's Haircolor Secrets
- Coloring African-American Hair
- Haircolor Consultation Skills
- How to Become a Recognized Haircolor Expert
- How to Make More Money Behind The Chair
- The Ultimate Salon Marketing Plan

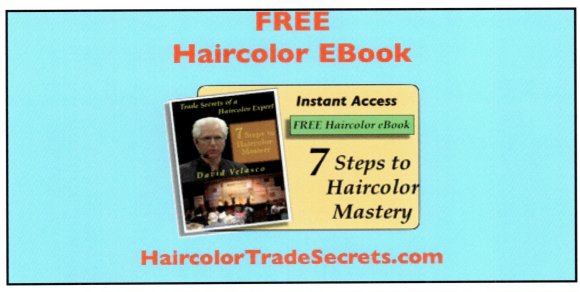

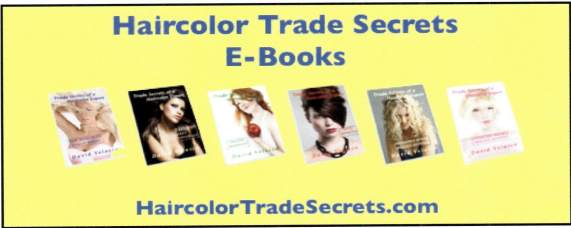

HAIRCOLOR TERMINOLOGY GLOSSARY

ACCELERATOR...(See ACTIVATOR)

ACCENT COLOR... A concentrated color product that can be added to permanent, semi-permanent or temporary haircolor to intensify or tone down the color. Another word for concentrate.

ACID.... An aqueous (water based) solution having a pH less than 7.0 on the pH scale.

ACTIVATOR... An additive used to quicken the action or progress of a chemical. Another word for booster, accelerator, protenator or catalyst.

ALKALINE.... An aqueous (water based) solution having a pH greater than 7.0 on the pH scale. The opposite of acid.

ALLERGY...... A physical reaction resulting from extreme sensitivity to exposure, contact and/or ingestion of certain foods or chemicals.

ALLERGY TEST... A test to determine the possibility or degree of sensitivity; also known as a patch test, predisposition test or skin test.

AMINO ACIDS.... The group of molecules that the body uses to synthesize protein. There are 22 different amino acids found in living protein that serve as units of structure.

AMMONIA.... A colorless pungent gas composed of hydrogen and nitrogen; in water solution is called ammonia water. Used in haircolor to swell the cuticle. When mixed with hydrogen peroxide, it activates the oxidation process on melanin, and allows the melanin to decolorize.
AMMONIUM HYDROXIDE..... An alkali solution of ammonia in water; commonly used in the manufacturing of permanent haircolor, lightener preparations and hair relaxers.

ANALYSIS (HAIR).... An examination of the hair to determine its condition and natural color. (SEE CONSULTATION, CONDITION)

AQUEOUS..... Descriptive term for water solution or any medium that is largely composed of water.

ASH... A tone or shade dominated by greens, blues, violets or grays. May be used to counteract unwanted warm tones.

BASE (ALKALI)... (See pH; ALKALINE)

BASE COLOR.... (See COLOR BASE)

BLEACH... (See LIGHTENER)

BLEEDING... Seepage of tint/lightener from the packet containing the hair to be colored or frosting cap due to improper application.

BLENDING.... A merging of one tint or tone with another.

BLONDING... A term applied to lightening the hair.

BONDS.... The means by which atoms are joined together to make molecules.

BOOSTER... (See ACTIVATOR)

BRASSY TONE... Undesirable red, orange or gold tones in the hair.

BREAKAGE... A condition in which hair splits and breaks off.

BUFFER ZONE... Applying color away from the scalp to avoid chemical overlapping.

BUILD-UP... Repeated coatings on the hair shaft.

BUMPING THE BASE... A term used to describe a gentle degree of lift of the natural color.

CATALYST... A substance used to alter the speed of a chemical reaction.

CATEGORY... A method of defining natural hair to help determine the undertones.

CAUSTIC... Strongly alkaline materials. At very high pH levels, can burn or destroy protein or tissue by chemical action.

CERTIFIED COLOR... A color which meets certain standards for purity and is certified by the FDA.

CERTIFIED HAIRCOLORIST.... A haircolorist who has passed a rigid examination process established by the American Board of Certified Haircolorists.

CETYL ALCOHOL... Fatty alcohol used as an emollient. It is also used as a stabilizer for emulsion systems, and in haircolor and cream developer as a thickener.

CHELATING STABILIZER.... A molecule that binds metal ions and renders them inactive.

CHEMICAL CHANGE... Alteration in the chemical composition of a substance.

CITRIC ACID.... Organic acid derived from citrus fruits and used for pH adjustment. Primarily used to adjust the acid-alkali balance. Has some antioxidant and preservative qualities. Used medicinally as a mild astringent.

COATING... Residue left on the outside of the hair shaft.

COLOR... Visual sensation caused by light.

COLOR ADDITIVE... (see ACCENT COLOR)

COLOR BASE... The combination of dyes which make up the tonal foundation of a specific haircolor.

COLOR LIFT... The amount of change natural or artificial pigment undergoes when lightened by a substance.

COLOR MIXING... Combining two or more shades together for a custom color.

COLOR REFRESHER... (1) Color applied to midshaft and ends to give a more uniform color appearance to the hair. (2) Color applied by a shampoo-in method to enhance the natural color. Also called color wash, color enhancer, color glaze.

COLOR REMOVER.... A product designed to remove artificial pigment from the hair.

COLOR TEST.... The process of removing product from a hair strand to monitor the progress of color development during tinting or lightening.

COLOR WHEEL.... The arrangement of primary, secondary and tertiary colors in the order of their relationships to each other. A tool for formulating.

COMPLEMENTARY COLORS... A primary and secondary color positioned opposite each other on the color wheel. When these two colors are combined, they create a neutral color. Combinations are as follows: Blue/Orange, Red/Green, Yellow/Violet.

CONCENTRATE... (See ACCENT COLOR)
CONDITION.... The existing state of the hair; its elasticity, strength, texture, porosity and evidence of previous treatments.

CONSULTATION.... Verbal communication with a client to determine desired result. [See ANALYSIS (HAIR)]

CONTRIBUTING PIGMENT... The current level and tone of the hair. Refers to both natural contributing pigment and decolorized (lightened) contributing pigment. (See UNDERTONE)

COOL TONES... (See ASH)

CORRECTIVE COLORING... The process of correcting an undesirable color.

CORTEX.... The second layer of hair. A fibrous protein core of the hair fiber, containing melanin pigment.

COVERAGE... Reference to the ability of a color product to color gray, white or other colors of hair.

CUTICLE.... The translucent, protein outer layer of the hair fiber.

CYSTEIC ACID.... A chemical substance in the hair fiber, produced by the interaction of hydrogen peroxide on the disulfide bond (cystine).

CYSTINE.... The disulfide amino acid, which joins protein chains together.

D & C COLORS.... Colors selected from a certified list approved by the Food and Drug Administration for use in drug and cosmetic products.

DECOLORIZE... A chemical process involving the lightening of the natural color pigment or artificial color from the hair.
DEGREE.... Term used to describe various units of measurement.

DEMI-COLOR... (See DEPOSIT-ONLY COLOR)

DENSE.... Thick, compact, or crowded.

DEPOSIT.... Describes the color product in terms of its ability to add color pigment to the hair. Color added equals deposit.

DEPOSIT-ONLY COLOR... A category of color products between permanent and semi-permanent colors. Formulated to only deposit color, not lift. They contain oxidative dyes and utilize a low volume developer.

DEPTH... The lightness or darkness of a specific haircolor. (See VALUE, LEVEL)

DEVELOPER.... An oxidizing agent, usually hydrogen peroxide that reacts chemically with coloring material to develop color molecules and create a change in natural haircolor.

DEVELOPMENT TIME (OXIDATION PERIOD).... The time required for a permanent color or lightener to completely develop.

DIFFUSED.... Broken down, scattered; not limited to one spot.

DIRECT DYE.... A preformed color that dyes the fiber directly without the need for oxidation.

DISCOLORATION... The development of undesired shades through chemical reaction.

DOUBLE PROCESS... A technique requiring two separate procedures in which the hair is decolorized or prelightened with a lightener, before the depositing color is applied.

DRAB... Term used to describe haircolor shades containing no red or gold. (See ASH, DULL)

DRABBER.... Concentrated color used to reduce red or gold highlights.

DULL.... A word used to describe hair or haircolor without sheen.

DYE.... Artificial pigment.

DYE INTERMEDIATE... A material, which develops into color only after reaction with developer (hydrogen peroxide). Also known as oxidation dyes.

DYE REMOVER (SOLVENTS)... (See COLOR REMOVER)

DYE STOCK.... (See COLOR BASE)

ELASTICITY... The ability of the hair to stretch and return too normal.

ENZYME... A protein molecule found in living cells which initiates a chemical process.

EUMELANIN...A dark brown to almost black color pigment that determines the depth of the hairs natural color. (Eumelanin and Pheomelanin are found in the cortex of the hair and are collectively known as Melanin)

FADE... To lose color through exposure to the elements or other factors.

FILLERS.... (1) Color product used as a color refresher or to replace undertones in damaged hair in preparation for haircoloring. (2) Any liquid-like substance to help fill the need for natural undertones. (See COLOR REFRESHER)

FORMULAS.... Mixture of two or more ingredients.

FORMULATE.... The art of mixing to create a blend or balance of two or more ingredients.

FROSTING... The introduction of lighter strands to the hair; generally executed with a frosting cap.

GLAZING... A term used to describe a translucent color used on the hair after a previous haircolor; a blending color.

GRAY HAIR. Hair with no natural pigment is actually white. White hairs look gray when mingled with pigmented hair.

HAIR..... A slender threadlike outgrowth on the skin of the head and body.

HAIR ROOT... That part of the hair contained within the follicle, below the surface of the scalp.

HAIR SHAFT.... Visible part of each strand of hair. It is made up of an outer layer called the cuticle, an innermost layer called medulla and an in-between layer called the cortex. The cortex layer is where color changes are made.

HARD WATER.... Water that contains minerals and metallic salts as impurities.

HENNA… A plant extracted coloring that produces bright shades of red. The active ingredient is lawsone. Henna permanently colors the hair by coating and penetrating the hair shaft. (See PROGRESSIVE DYE)

HIGH LIFT TINTING... A single process color with a higher degree of lightening action and a minimal amount of color deposit.

HIGHLIGHTING.... The introduction of a lighter color in small selected sections to increase lightness of the hair.

HYDROGEN PEROXIDE... An oxidizing chemical made up of 2 parts hydrogen, 2 parts oxygen ($H2O2$) used to aid the processing of permanent haircolor and lighteners. Also referred to as a developer; available in liquid or cream.

LEVEL... A unit of measurement used to evaluate the lightness or darkness of a color, excluding tone.

LEVEL SYSTEM... In haircoloring, a system colorists use to analyze the lightness or darkness of a haircolor.

LIFT.... The lightening action of a haircolor or lightening product on the hair's natural pigment.

LIGHTENER... The chemical compound which lightens the hair by dispersing, dissolving and decolorizing the natural hair pigment. (See PRE-LIGHTEN)

LIGHTENING.... (See DECOLORIZE)

LINE OF DEMARCATION... An obvious difference between two colors on the hair shaft.

LITMUS PAPER... A chemically treated paper used to test the acidity or alkalinity of products.

MEDULLA... The center structure of the hair shaft. Very little is known about its actual function.

MELANIN.... The tiny grains of pigment in the hair cortex which create natural haircolor.

MELANOCYTES... Cells in the hair bulb that manufacture melanin.

MELANOPROTEIN.... The protein coating of melanosome.

METALLIC DYES.... Soluble metal salts such as lead, silver and bismuth produce colors on the hair fiber, by progressive build-up and exposure to air.

MODIFIER.... A chemical found as an ingredient in permanent haircolors. Its function is to alter the dye intermediates.

MOLECULE... Two or more atoms chemically joined together; the smallest part of a compound.

NEUTRAL... (1) A color balanced between warm and cool, which does not reflect a highlight of any primary or secondary color. (2) Also refers to a pH of 7.

NEUTRALIZATION... The process that counter-balances or cancels the action of an agent or color.

NEUTRALIZE... Render neutral; counter-balance of action or influence. (See NEUTRAL)

NEW GROWTH... The part of the hair shaft that is between previously chemically treated hair and the scalp.

NONALKALINE.... (See ACID)

OFF THE SCALP LIGHTENER... Generally a stronger lightener (usually in powder form), not to be used directly on the scalp.

ON THE SCALP LIGHTENER... A liquid, cream or gel form of lightener that can be used directly on the scalp.

OPAQUE.... Allowing no light to shine through; flat; lack of translucency.

OUT GROWTH... (See NEW GROWTH)

OVER-LAP... Occurs when the application of color or lightener goes beyond the line of demarcation.

OVER POROUS... The condition where hair reaches an undesirable stage of porosity requiring correction.

OXIDATION.... (1) The reaction of dye intermediates with hydrogen peroxide found in haircoloring developers. (2) The interaction of hydrogen peroxide on the natural pigment.

OXIDATIVE HAIRCOLOR.... A product containing oxidation dyes which require hydrogen peroxide to develop the permanent color.

PARA TINT... A tint made from oxidation dyes.

PARA-PHENYLENEDIAMINE... An oxidative dye used in most permanent haircolors, often abbreviated as P.P.D.

PATCH TEST.... A test required by the Food and Drug Act. Performed by applying a small amount of the haircoloring preparation to the skin of the arm, or behind the ear to determine possible allergies (hypersensitivity). Also called pre- disposition or skin test.

PENETRATING COLOR.... Color that penetrates the cortex or second layer of the hair shaft.

PERMANENT COLOR.... (1) Haircolor products that do not wash out by shampooing. (2) A category of haircolor products mixed with developer that create a lasting color change.

PEROXIDE... (See HYDROGEN PEROXIDE)

PEROXIDE RESIDUE.... Traces of peroxide left in the hair after treatment with lightener or tint.

PERSULFATE.... In haircoloring, a chemical ingredient commonly used in activators that increases the speed of the decolorization process. (See ACTIVATOR)

pH.... The quantity that expresses the acid/alkali balance. A pH of 7 is the neutral value for pure water. Any pH below 7 is acidic; any pH above 7 is alkaline. The skin is mildly acidic, and generally in the pH 4.5 to 5.5 range.

pH SCALE... A numerical scale from 0 (very acid) to 14 (very alkaline), used to describe the degree of acidity or alkalinity.

PHEOMELANIN... Red and Yellow pigments that give the hair warmth to the natural color. (Eumelanin and Pheomelanin are found in the cortex of the hair and are collectively known as Melanin)

PIGMENT.... Any substance or matter used as coloring; natural or artificial haircolor.

POROSITY.... Ability of the hair to absorb water or other liquids.

POWDER LIGHTENER... (See OFF THE SCALP LIGHTENER)

PREBLEACHING ... (See PRELIGHTEN)

PREDISPOSITION TEST.... (See PATCH TEST)

PRELIGHTEN.... Generally, the first step of double process haircoloring. To lift or lighten the natural pigment. (See DECOLORIZE)

PRESOFTEN.... The process of treating gray or very resistant hair to allow for better penetration of color.

PRIMARY COLORS... Pigments or colors that are fundamental and cannot be made by mixing colors together. Red, yellow and blue are the primary colors.

PRISM.... A transparent glass or crystal that breaks up white light into its component colors -the spectrum.

PROCESSING TIME.... The time required for the chemical treatment to react on the hair.

PROGRESSIVE DYES OR PROGRESSIVE DYE SYSTEM... (1) A coloring system which produces increased absorption with each application. (2) Color products that deepen or increase absorption over a period of time during processing.

REGROWTH.... (See NEW GROWTH)

RESISTANT HAIR... Hair that is difficult to penetrate with moisture or chemical solutions.

RETOUCH.... Application of color or lightening mixture to new growth of hair.

SALT AND PEPPER... The descriptive term for a mixture of dark and gray or white hair.

SECONDARY COLOR... Colors made by combining two primary colors in equal proportion; green, orange and violet are secondary colors.

SEMI-PERMANENT HAIRCOLORING.... A pre-oxidized haircolor requiring no catalyst that lasts through several shampoos. It stains the cuticle layer, slowly fading with each shampoo.

SENSITIVITY... Skin that is highly reactive to the presence of a specific chemical. Skin reddens or becomes irritated shortly after application of the chemical. The reaction subsides when the chemical has been removed.

SHADE... (1) A term used to describe a specific color. (2) The visible difference between two colors.

SHEEN.... The ability of the hair to shine, gleam or reflect light.

SINGLE PROCESS COLOR... Refers to an oxidative tint solution that lifts or lightens, while also depositing color in one application.
(See OXIDATIVE HAIRCOLOR)

SOFTENING AGENT... A mild alkaline product applied prior to the color treatment to increase porosity, swell the cuticle layer of the hair and increase color absorption. Tint that has not been mixed with developer is frequently used. (See PRE-SOFTEN)

SOLUTION... A blended mixture of solid, liquid or gaseous substances in a liquid medium.

SOLVENT... Carrier liquid in which other components may be dissolved.

SPECIALIST.... One who concentrates on only one part or branch of a subject or profession.

SPECTRUM.... The series of colored bands diffracted and arranged in the order of their wavelengths by the passage of white light through a prism. Shading continuously from red (produced by the longest wave visible) to violet (produced by the shortest):red, orange, yellow, green, blue, indigo and violet.

SPOT LIGHTENING... Color correcting using a lightening mixture to lighten darker areas.

STABILIZER... General name for ingredient, which prolongs life, appearance and performance of a product.

STAGE... A term used to describe a visible color change that natural haircolor goes through while being lightened.

STAIN REMOVER... Chemical used to remove tint stains from skin.

STRAND TEST... Test given before treatment to determine development time, color result and the ability of the hair to withstand the effects of chemicals.

STRIPPING... (See COLOR REMOVER)

SURFACTANT.... An abbreviation for Surface Active Agent. A molecule which is composed of an oil-loving (oleophillic) part and a water-loving (hydrophilic) part. They act as a bridge to allow oil and water to mix. Wetting agents, emulsifiers, cleansers, solubilizers, dispersing aids and thickeners are usually surfactants.

TABLESPOON.... 1/2 ounce; 2 teaspoons.

TEASPOON.... 1/6 ounce; 1/2 of a tablespoon.

TEMPORARY COLOR OR RINSES.... Color made from preformed dyes that are applied to the hair for short-term effect. This type of product is readily removed with shampoo.

TERMINOLOGY.... The special words or terms used in science, art or business.

TERTIARY COLORS.... The mixture of a primary and an adjacent secondary color on the color wheel. red-orange, yellow-orange, yellow-green, blue-green, blue-violet, red-violet. Also referred to as intermediary colors.

TEXTURE, HAIR.... The diameter of an individual hair strand. Termed: coarse, medium or fine.

TINT.... Permanent oxidizing haircolor product, having the ability to lift and deposit color in the same process. Requires a developer.

TINT BACK... To return hair back to its original or natural color.

TONE... A term used to describe the warmth or coolness in color.

TONER... A pastel color to be used after pre-lightening.

TONING. Adding color to modify the end result.
TOUCH-UP... (See RETOUCH)

TRANSLUCENT... The property of letting diffused light pass through.

TYROSINE.... The amino acid (tyrosine), which reacts together with the enzyme (tyrosinase) to form the hairs natural melanin.

TYROSINASE... The enzyme (tyrosinase) which reacts together with the amino acid (tyrosine) to form the hairs natural melanin.

UNDERTONE... The underlying color in melanin that emerges during the lifting process and contributes to the end result. When lightening hair, a residual warmth in tone always occurs.

UREA PEROXIDE... A peroxide compound occasionally used in haircolor. It releases oxygen when added to an alkaline color mixture.

VALUE.... (See LEVEL; DEPTH)

VEGETABLE COLOR.... A color derived from plant sources.

VIRGIN HAIR.... Natural hair that has not undergone any chemical or physical abuse.

VISCOSITY... A term referring to the thickness of a solution.

VOLUME.... The concentration of hydrogen peroxide in water solution. Expressed as volumes of oxygen liberated per volume of solution. 20 volume peroxide would thus liberate 20 pints of oxygen gas for each pint of solution.

WARM... A term used to describe haircolor. Containing red, orange, yellow or gold tones.

Collect the Full Series

and Create Your Own

Haircolor Education Library

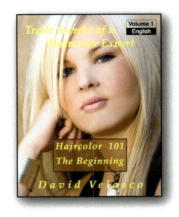

Trade Secrets of a Haircolor Expert — Volume 1 English
Haircolor 101 The Beginning
David Velasco

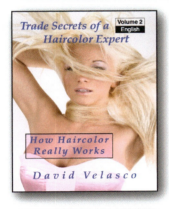

Trade Secrets of a Haircolor Expert — Volume 2 English
How Haircolor Really Works
David Velasco

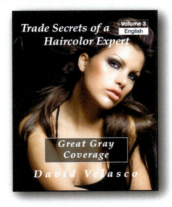

Trade Secrets of a Haircolor Expert — Volume 3 English
Great Gray Coverage
David Velasco

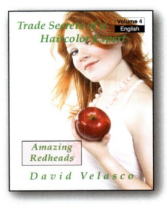

Trade Secrets of a Haircolor Expert — Volume 4 English
Amazing Redheads
David Velasco

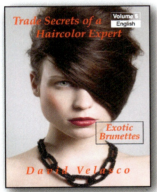

Trade Secrets of a Haircolor Expert — Volume 5 English
Exotic Brunettes
David Velasco

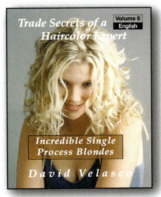

Trade Secrets of a Haircolor Expert — Volume 6 English
Incredible Single Process Blondes
David Velasco

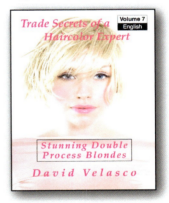

Trade Secrets of a Haircolor Expert — Volume 7 English
Stunning Double Process Blondes
David Velasco

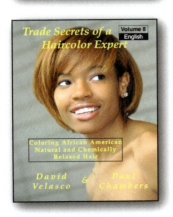

Trade Secrets of a Haircolor Expert — Volume 8 English
Coloring African American Natural and Chemically Relaxed Hair
David Velasco & Paul Chambers

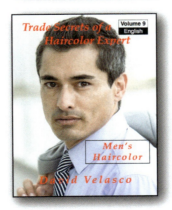

Trade Secrets of a Haircolor Expert — Volume 9 English
Men's Haircolor
David Velasco

Trade Secrets of a Haircolor Expert — Volume 10 English
101 Trade Secrets of a Haircolor Consultation
David Velasco

David Velasco

- *HAIRCOLOR SPECIALIST*
- *MASTER STYLIST*
- *SALON OWNER*
- *EDUCATOR*
- *CONSULTANT*
- *AUTHOR*

With 40 years Experience in the field of hairdressing, Velasco has become one of the industry's leading authorities.

Velasco began his career at the young age of 16 in Tampa.Fla. He soon moved to London, England where he worked and studied his craft with world-renowned hairdressers of that era.

Upon return to the USA Velasco began to develop his skills as an Educator and Effective Communicator while working with John & Suzzane Chadwick at the "Hair Fashion Development Center" on New York's 5th Ave.

By the age of 21 Velasco was STYLES DIRECTOR for the SAKS FIFTH AVE. beauty salon in New York City. Over the next 20 years Velasco became involved in almost every aspect of hair related activities possible. Including such achievements as, Freelance Hair Designer for photo sessions with major beauty publications and television commercials. He has held such prestige positions as Educational and Creative Consultant to CLAIROL INC., SHISEIDO LTD.,& THE WELLA CORP..

He has preformed as the Featured Guest Artist and Master Educator at hundreds of trade events throughout the world. His presentation at HAIRCOLOR U.S.A., symposium was rated BEST EDUCATIONAL EVENT by his peers.

Velasco has been a Contributing Author to many hair related articles for both consumer and professional publications and books. Velasco held a position as the NATIONAL ARTISTIC DIRECTOR FOR THE WELLA CORP. for ten years and is a member of the INTERNATIONAL HAIRCOLOR EXCHANGE.

Velasco was formally the DIRECTOR OF HAIRCOLOR for the world renowned BUMBLE & BUMBLE SALON in NEW YORK CITY and presently resides over his own salon David Velasco Salon, LTD. in Doylestown, Pennsylvania.

David and his Salon are proud members of INTERCOIFFURE MONDIAL, which is the most prestigious international hairdressing organization in the world.

As an industry leader, David is also owner of "Salon Success Systems Publications" through which he has Authored and Self-Published many books in the Art of Haircolor branded: **"Trade Secrets of a Haircolor Expert",** and produced a Series of Educational DVD's and a social networking website:**"The Haircolor Clubhouse"** where he provides free haircolor education to professional hairdressers around the world.

CPSIA information can be obtained at www.ICGtesting.com
Printed in the USA
LVIW01n1614060317
526285LV00011B/157